Teen Voices
Real Teens Discuss
Real Problems™

Teens Talk About
Self-Esteem and
Self-Confidence

Edited by Jennifer Landau

Featuring Q&As with Teen Health & Wellness's Dr. Jan

Rosen
YA™
New York

Published in 2018 by The Rosen Publishing Group, Inc.
29 East 21st Street, New York, NY 10010

First Edition

Library of Congress Cataloging-in-Publication Data

Names: Landau, Jennifer, 1961–editor.
Title: Teens talk about self-esteem and self-confidence / edited by Jennifer Landau.
Description: New York: Rosen Publishing, 2018 | Series: Teen voices: real teens discuss real problems | Includes bibliographical references and index. | Audience: Grades 7–12.
Identifiers: LCCN 2017019726| ISBN 9781508176534 (library bound) | ISBN 9781508176619 (pbk.) | ISBN 9781508176374 (6 pack)
Subjects: LCSH: Self-esteem in adolescence. | Self-confidence in adolescence. | Teenagers.
Classification: LCC BF724.3.S36 T44 2018 | DDC 155.5/182—dc23
LC record available at https://lccn.loc.gov/2017019726

Manufactured in China

The content in this title has been compiled from The Rosen Publishing Group's Teen Health & Wellness digital platform. Additional original content was provided by Lisa A. Crayton.

Contents

Introduction

As a growing teen, you have already witnessed change in your physical development, in academic settings, and in society as a whole. Without a doubt, change happens daily. And every day brings its share of successes and setbacks.

Self-esteem and self-confidence play a role in how you respond to those daily triumphs and disappointments. Self-esteem is your perception of yourself. It includes your thoughts, opinions, and feelings. Someone with low self-esteem has negative thoughts about himself, which comes through in how he talks about his body, intellect, or abilities.

For instance, comments like, "I'm so dumb," "There's nothing special about me," and "No one likes me" are indicators that a teen's self-esteem needs boosting. So is a preoccupation with losing weight or gaining muscle that compels her to stop eating or to use steroids. Conversely, easily accepting her not-so-perfect body parts without speaking negatively about them is a sign of someone with healthy self-esteem.

Exercise is a healthy way to improve your physical and emotional well-being, but a preoccupation with weight may indicate your self-esteem needs a boost.

Self-confidence stems from self-esteem. Among other things, it is reflected in how a teen walks, talks, and treats others. For example, teens with healthy self-confidence do not engage in self-harm activities. Self-confident teens also project a "can do" attitude that is contagious. They try new things and inspire other teens to do the same.

Teen boys and girls can struggle with self-esteem and self-confidence issues. Self-esteem and self-confidence affects:

Share Your Own Story

The stories you are about to read were submitted by your peers to the Teen Health & Wellness Personal Story Project. Sharing stories is a powerful way to connect with other people. By sharing your story, you can connect with others who are dealing with these challenges. Find more information about how to submit your own story at the end of this resource.

- How you deal with real or perceived imperfections
- Your posture
- Your willingness to try new things
- The way you respond to criticisms and compliments
- Whether you are socially active or isolate yourself from friends and relatives.

Many teens could benefit from improved self-esteem or self-confidence. It's possible to improve both so that you are willing and able to face yourself, other people, and the world! There are five major areas that teens can work on to make that happen:

1. Standing up for themselves
2. Overcoming a negative self-image
3. Facing fears
4. Finding themselves through creative expression
5. Helping others to help themselves

Teens struggling with self-esteem and self-confidence issues often isolate themselves from family and friends, even when they long to have an active social life.

Making adjustments in one or more of these areas will boost a teen's self-esteem and self-confidence. While addressing issues may be uncomfortable, ignoring them could have dire consequences. Cutting oneself, social isolation, academic failures, and even suicide can be traced, in part, to a teen's unresolved esteem and/or confidence issues.

On the other hand, improved self-regard, academic success, and emotional well-being result when a teen's self-esteem and self-confidence soar. When self-esteem and self-confidence rises, a teen finds the courage to be her authentic self, the one that is visible and present when she is both alone and with others: the one that shines through at home, in classrooms, and throughout the community.

Chapter 1

Teens Talk About Standing Up for Themselves

Some teens pick on their peers about anything and everything. Others make up stuff just to ridicule their siblings, friends, or classmates. These bullies often put down another teen's positive qualities, such as his kind personality, or stellar test scores. They belittle classmates, neighbors, and strangers just to make those people feel small or inferior.

That is likely no surprise to you. According to Pacer's National Bullying Prevention Center twenty percent of students have reported being bullied. Bullying poses serious physical, emotional, and mental risks to affected teens. It also adds to the stress teens already face, which is significant.

In a 2013 survey by the American Psychological Association, more than 25 percent of responding teens reported feeling "extreme" stress during the school term. Meanwhile, in Canada, 42 percent of teens responding to a 2015 survey by Kids Help Phone said they were stressed.

Bullies use public places like school cafeterias to pick on classmates, bar them from conversations, and further belittle victims in front of other students.

Criticism, like bullying, is rampant in schools. But teens also face it at home and other places they go. Depending on the day, those comments can hurt or infuriate. Almost every day, though, those remarks send self-esteem and self-confidence plummeting.

What to do? Learn how to assert yourself in the face of criticism and bullying. Work on valuing your own opinion over other people's opinions and speak out when you're being bullied. These techniques can help you free yourself from a negative self-image when confronted with criticism and cruel behavior.

Emoijah's Story

Got Self-Esteem?

"How old are you?"

It was in the middle of Psychology class when a girl asked me that same question. She was sitting across from me, her eyebrows arching up with curiosity.

"Fifteen," I answered.

Her eyes widened and her mouth formed into a bubble until she resembled a blowfish. I realized she was trying to stifle her giggling, but it didn't work. She erupted in laughter and stared at me.

"Really?" she asked, flabbergasted.

"Yes," I frowned. "How old do I look?"

"Twelve." The word barely escaped from her throat before the snickering continued.

What? I thought. I look like I'm twelve? I sank back into my seat, ashamed as I stared at my fingers. I wanted to say something so bad, defend myself, make a comeback—just do something.

But I just sat there and continued to dwell on the insult. It really wasn't the first time something like that made me feel humiliated. My former classmates and "friends" commented disapprovingly on my hair, the clothes I wore, or the things I did.

Each and every time they made a criticism— even when it was not meant to "bully" or be unaccommodating—the words devoured me, taking a bite out of my self-esteem and pride as I constantly thought about it.

Other people's opinions and negative comments will rock your self-confidence unless you learn to focus on what makes you special and unique.

So there I was, staring at the other person across the mirror, scrutinizing her every flaw (which I thought was just about everything). I never bothered to see that it was all a question of my own self-pride. Although I put a dark cloud of negativity about myself, I did think, all the time, "Why should I care what people think about me, anyway?"

However, the rhetorical question was just as thoughtless as the old saying: "Sticks and stones may break my bones, but words will never hurt me."

I was very sensitive, but I knew that even if I developed some "thick skin," that would obviously not erase the problem. Honestly, the problem was never other people's words, but how I took them in.

So, desperately needing a lift in my own dignity, I ran to a close friend of mine.

"Jade," I said. "Do you see anything wrong with me?" As we were sitting together on the bus like good old friends, I passed the question along casually.

"What?" She frowned at me.

"Do you see anything wrong with me? Like my hair— you know, stuff like that?"

Jade was still staring at me in utter bewilderment. "No, there's nothing wrong with you. Why?"

"Honestly?"

"Yes," she said. She narrowed her eyes at me. "Why are you even asking me this, anyway?"

I sat back with a little bit of relief. "Nothing," I breathed.

Days later when I finally explained the situation to her, she told me not to worry about what people say. In my head, I was dumbfounded. How do I NOT worry about what people say? I'm sensitive, remember?

"You know, people used to make fun of me and told me I was fat," Jade told me.

I frowned as I knew she was not fat. "Well, what did you do?"

"I was upset for a long while, you know, and did some stupid stuff so I was kind of anorexic."

Talking to a trusted friend or adult helps put things in perspective and gives a teen the chance to see himself in a different light.

We listened to each other and I realized how puerile the things we were slamming ourselves for were.

"I like your hair—it's nice," she responded to my silly statement about my "messed-up" hair. When I could finally laugh about the whole affair, I thought: Why do we look at all our "imperfections" and not the things that make us special?

The following week after the whole "You're fifteen?!" scenario, I decided to lift my head up and just joke about it. I came to the conclusion that walking around with my head down and making myself look "vulnerable" wouldn't help me in the least.

So, from that point on, I held my head up high and walked with a lot of pride, happy not to be my "insulters" but my own self. And you know what? No one ever said anything to me since—well, huh, if they did, I laughed about it. Hey, my self-esteem was much higher than theirs, anyway.

Don't let anybody ever get under your skin when it comes to bullying or criticizing you, because at the end of the day the only thing that matters is what you think. Honestly.

Natalie's Story

While I was growing up, I used to live in an environment where it was all right for one person to ridicule and degrade another. I was one of the many victims of bullying, by both the people I called friends and the people I thought I could call family.

The words "fat," "ugly," and "disgusting" were just a few words that seemed to linger in my head after a long day of abuse. "Playfulness" seemed to be the word many people called their actions, claiming that they were "just kidding" and that they "didn't mean it."

My self-esteem was almost non-existent for as long as I could remember. The fear that took over my body every time I would try to stand up for myself almost felt unreal. My throat felt constricted, and my head would instantly face the ground, and my mouth never seemed to want to open. The constant tightness in my chest made it ache as I took the harsh words and the painful shoves into the dirt. I couldn't fight back. I was afraid that if I did, the abuse that was directed at me would be passed onto someone else. No one should have to deal with such cruelty, and the thought of other people feeling like I did was too painful to imagine. Not only that—I was afraid that if I didn't put up with the harshness of these people, I was somehow letting down the ones I truly cared for. When I finally did tell someone, however, I realized that that wasn't the case.

One day, it seemed that my mind had had enough abuse and something inside me broke. It took me a few hours to actually gather up enough courage, but after a good pep talk and a few deep breaths, I finally told the one person I knew who would believe me. I explained to my mother about how I was bullied at school and at home by the other children in the family. I came clean about all of the name calling, and the pushing and the shoving. Every word that came out of my mouth seemed to loosen up the tightness in my chest and for the first time in forever—I could breathe. It felt so good to tell someone my struggles, to talk to someone who cared. To say my mother was furious would be an understatement.

A few months later, I started living with my grandmother. She welcomed me with open arms and helped me begin the process of regaining the confidence I had lost. The new school I had been enrolled in took me by surprise. They had many policies against bullying that somehow made me feel safer than I did at the last school I went to. The people that attended

Standing up for yourself sometimes means letting go of old friends and finding new friends who have your best interests at heart.

and worked there were nice and cheerful. I had finally made friends who I could actually call my friends. They treated me like a person, and they cared about my well-being in a way that was foreign to me at the time. I am honored to say that we are all still friends to this day.

I can proudly state that I am glad I told someone about the cycle I was trapped in. Today, I can get up and attend school without being surrounded by people who enjoy putting down others. I can laugh and joke around with my friends, and I can return home to a family that loves and supports me. I'm no longer trapped in a cocoon of self-loathing and fear.

I can truly be myself. No more restrictions, no more walls, no more getting up after being pushed down. I'm free, truly and utterly free, and honestly it's the best feeling in the world.

MYTHS AND FACTS

MYTH   The "popular kids" do not suffer from poor self-esteem.

FACT   A person's popularity is not a true measure of self-esteem or self-confidence.

MYTH   A person can grow out of low self-esteem as they get older.

FACT   Self-esteem is not based on age. If a person doesn't take action or get help, he or she may continue to suffer with self-esteem and self-confidence issues throughout life.

MYTH   If you have tried before but failed to improve your self-esteem it is not worth trying again.

FACT   You deserve to have healthy self-esteem and self-confidence. Get help developing an action plan that will help you maintain long-term growth in these areas.

Chapter 2

Teens Talk About Overcoming a Negative Self-Image

What is attractiveness? Is it limited to outer appearance, including things like facial features, hair, body shape, weight, height, and physical abilities? Some teens are quick to label another person unappealing based on those factors. But beauty is in the eye of the beholder. If that teen were placed in a different culture some of those same attributes would be considered highly attractive.

Teens should not limit their definition of beauty to what they see in the mirror because physical appearance is not the only thing that makes someone attractive.

There is no universal definition of beauty, despite advertisements that seem to indicate otherwise. Strength, courage, resilience, helpfulness, and other characteristics play a role in whether a person sees someone else as handsome or beautiful.

Your image of yourself has a great impact on how others see you. If you see yourself as unattractive physically or browbeat yourself because of a perceived or real weakness, you will suffer from a poor self-image. You will feel unattractive and avoid people and possibly engage in self-destructive behavior.

Taking positive steps to overcome a poor self-image can help. To build up your sense of self try taking the following steps:

- Accept your perceived imperfections while working on improving your mental or physical health.
- Sign up for free tutoring in subjects you need help with.
- Admit and get help for eating or anxiety disorders—getting help is a sign of strength, not weakness.
- Eat more nutritious meals and snacks.
- Walk, swim, play sports, or get other daily or weekly exercise to boost your overall physical health.
- Make friends with teens who display self-confidence because of their positive self-image.
- Talk positively about you *to* you. This "self-talk" about your body, abilities, or feelings can boost self-esteem and confidence.

These are all practical, doable steps. Long term, they will help you overcome a poor self-image and enjoy a brighter future than you ever imagined.

Kenna's Story

Ever since I was in fourth grade, I have hated myself. I felt unattractive because of my weight. Being a chubby girl and wanting to fit in is hard. I always put myself down and held myself back because I didn't want to be made fun of or embarrass myself. Over the years I tried to lose weight, forever dreaming of that perfect body to show off. The months and years passed by, and my body was only getting heavier and heavier. I fell into a dark hole of self-hatred. I wondered why I was so ugly and untalented.

It wasn't until I was in seventh grade that I realized I had to change. The situation had become so bad that I would decline invitations to hang out with other girls because I was so embarrassed, and then I would spend my time at home crying because I thought I was hideous. I decided I should spend a lot less time worrying about my weight and more time building up my confidence in myself.

The changes came slowly, but surely. Sometimes I would slip when I looked into the mirror, but those days became fewer. I listened to songs about confidence. I cherished compliments I received instead of thinking they were lies. It also helped to compliment other people. One night I was in my bed crying, but my mom came in and told me how wonderful I was. Today I enjoy putting on pretty clothes and makeup, even though my size has not shrunk. I take care of myself by exercising and eating healthy because being healthy also gives me confidence.

Eating disorders can be a consequence of negative self-esteem and are not easily overcome without guidance from an adult who can provide useful tools, including nutrition advice.

It makes me sad to see girls go where I have gone. That deep, dark hole of self-hatred. It isn't worth it to be in there. It will only lead to things like anorexia or self-harm. You may not believe it, but you are worth it. You are beautiful. My philosophy is everyone is pretty, and everyone has at least one likable quality. Don't listen to any negativity, whether it be from yourself or others. Do things that make you feel happy and confident. Nobody truly cares how much you weigh. They really don't. I promise.

Meg's Story

There really wasn't anything special about this day. But I, as you should know, have always had an extensive imagination, and invented all sorts of subtle psychological reasons for why he did what he did. He smiled at me, and I smiled back. I wanted to pretend that it was more than that: that he had some real meaning in that smile and that maybe he loved me as much as I loved him.

Since kindergarten, we knew each other's names, yet it meant nothing. For me, that changed in middle school, and suddenly, I convinced myself that I was a skateboarder (I had a very good imagination, remember). That was why I wore DC wristbands everyday. I made it my daily goal to say hi to him, and to maybe, if I was lucky, strike up a conversation with him. I don't think I ever reached that goal.

My Latin teacher sent me a note from him once. We used dry-erase boards from class to class. The top of mine had all sorts of foreign markings on the top. "I think he was trying to write in Japanese to you," my Latin teacher said, as he shrugged with disinterest. The scribbles made me blush in delight. I dreamed that he had attempted to write *aishiteru*. That means "I love you" in Japanese. My friends said he had tried to call me after class, but I didn't hear. It was ironic, I suppose. Yet I was too shy to go find him later. Always too shy.

The end of the day was coming, so everyone sat in their seats and chattered. His voice called me from across the room. "Meg! Guess what. I can count to ten in Japanese!" Startled by the sudden conversation, directed at me no less, and the grin across his face, I couldn't help but watch him in awe. In that moment, I wished more than ever that I could spill out a stream of Japanese words back to him. Maybe he'd keep smiling at me. Maybe he'd even like me back.

Now did he see these moments the way I did? When he talked to me, was it because I was a friend or because he wanted to be more than that? I still don't know, but I wish I did. Sometimes, I think about him again, and wonder what would have happened if I told him I loved him. Would he have liked it? Would he have gotten as far away from me as he could in our tiny school? If I could go back there now, with the confidence I've gained, would something different have happened?

Whether he knew it or not, he gave me confidence. He was the one who asked me to sing a song, or who looked at what I was drawing. He made me want to show what I was thinking, be who I was, sing my own

True friends support one another and take an interest in each other's hobbies, including creative pursuits such as painting.

song. He made me proud to speak in Japanese, even if others laughed and told me to speak in English. He reminded me to be me. But I only realized that when he was gone. Ironically, it was only after we separated schools that I had the confidence to whisper to paper, "aishiteru."

Chapter 3

Teens Talk About Facing Their Fears

Fear is a powerful, destructive emotion. It affects people of all ages. Many things can trigger fear. Some common things people are afraid of include the sight of blood, heights, insects, air travel, public speaking, and performing in front of an audience. Some fear is grounded in a negative experience—you may have been bitten by a dog, so you now fear dogs. Other fear is based on "what if" scenarios that people imagine might happen, but which may never occur. For example, some people are afraid of getting on a boat or cruise ship because they worry it might sink.

Fear is often disruptive. Left unchecked it hinders a person's ability to enjoy everyday life. Gradually facing your fear is one way to overcome it. For example, if you fear speaking in front of crowds, taking a public speaking class can provide a safe place to learn skills and practice in front of smaller audiences. If you find it impossible to overcome any fear, seek help from a trusted adult, guidance counselor, or mental health professional.

Facing your fears can be liberating. It frees you up to do other things with your time. It allows you to

If a fear of flying prevents you from getting on an airplane, it can negatively impact your life. Learning to face a fear takes time and effort but can open up a world of possibilities.

experience life at its fullest without always worrying about what might happen. In addition, facing a particular fear builds confidence and self-esteem. In turn, greater confidence and self-esteem will empower you to face other fears, now or in the future.

Anh's Story

I love singing in the shower. There's nothing better than belting out those notes in the presence of honorable guests like bottles of shampoo and bars of soap. The water running out of the showerhead is a like a big pat on the back (or a million tiny ones), and the towels hang in awe from their bars. If my neighbors aren't sure of the idea already, they might guess that I have a passion for singing. Frankly, they wouldn't be wrong.

I'm not afraid of singing when it comes to facing the walls of my bathroom. But when I have to take a step out of the enclosed, private room and stand in front of a plethora of eyes staring into my soul, batteries fully charged and ready to judge, I feel the urge to run home and look at those labels on the bottles again. Fortunately, I am learning to slowly purge the fear. I even got a thrill out of showing my talent in front of people.

However, like many stories about stage fright, that wasn't the case for me in middle school.

I had auditioned for the school talent show in hopes of getting a bit of recognition for my passion. I passed, thankfully, but my glee was short-lived when I realized I was actually going to sing in front of the whole school (I clearly didn't think things through when putting my name on the sign-up sheet). Despite the ominous stage, I brushed things aside and put time into practicing. I practiced as much as I could without neglecting my schoolwork. As a result, the song I was going to sing somehow made its way into my dreams.

Of course, because time moves forward, the big day came.

The gym of my school suddenly grew four times bigger when I stepped inside. The jitters were finally catching up to me. I didn't want to be anywhere near the stage, so I took on the task of helping set up chairs for the audience across the gym. On a normal day, the job might have been monotonous to me, but that day, I couldn't help thinking about every person that who would be sitting in the chairs I set down, with their eyes and ears observing the show. As it got closer to the start of the show and I ran backstage to get ready, I found it extremely difficult to block out the sounds of everyone taking their seats.

What would they think of me?

What if I messed up?

Did my voice sound better in my head than it actually was?

Would people mock me?

Was I going to be labeled a "wannabe" singer?

Would there be disappointment?

What if no one clapped?

I stood in my corner, letting myself succumb to the negative thoughts. What was even worse was that I had signed up to perform willingly. I wanted someone to strongly encourage me or coerce me into standing in front of the school so it felt like I was putting my heart out there for someone. I wanted to walk out or find some excuse to stay off the stage. I wanted to run home and see the bottles of shampoo lining the window and the towels hanging patiently from their spots. But I couldn't do it because that would feel like I was being a traitor to myself. In my mind, I was running across a long distance to each option.

As I was starting to tire, the show had started, forcing my decision about whether to stay or leave.

The butterflies never flew out of my stomach, and my hands never stopped shaking as each performance took place on the other side of the curtain, but I mimicked what everyone else did and put on a smile.

I wasn't going to step down.

If I was capable of starting, I was capable of finishing.

I could do it, and I would do it.

Throughout my wait, I played every inspirational quote I knew of through my head. As I heard my name being called, I took that jump.

Many singers admit to having stage fright before each show, but they bravely face their fears and perform before an audience.

And flashing forward to present time, I'm still taking more jumps. I love the small space of my bathroom, but I know I will find a better sense of myself on the expansive stage. Next step: actually moving and singing at the same time instead of resembling a statue. Kidding. That came naturally.

Jessica's Story

"Are you sure you want to do this?"

My heart pounded. No, I was definitely not sure I wanted to do this.

"Yes," I responded quickly, before my mind could get the better of me. "Let's go."

"Do you want to look down at the slope first to make sure?" My father was hesitant and for good reason. It was my first time skiing in nearly seven years.

The Rocky Mountains were brutal and treacherous. One bad fall could twist your ankle or knee, if not worse. This course, in particular, was one of the harder double blues. It was steeper—and scarier—than anything else I had ever been down before. I may have walked away if it hadn't been my last day skiing before returning home. Today, however, was my last chance. I was going down that slope.

"No." I said, feeling determined. "I'll just psych myself out. Come on, let's go."

With a sigh, my father acquiesced. I led onward, ignoring my racing heart as my skis pointed themselves downward for my decline. Don't look past a few feet in front of you, I told myself as I slowly, carefully swayed back and forth down the mountain. The slope went

If you haven't taken part in a sport such as skiing for a long time, you may feel frightened your first time back on the slopes. But dealing with those fears is the only way to reconnect with an activity you enjoy.

downhill for what seemed to be miles, and I knew if I dared look up, I would be terrified. I took several deep breaths, watching only the snow directly in front of me. A few feet at a time. Just take it a few feet at a time. Keep calm, Jess.

I fought the urge to panic as the wind clouded my vision with an influx of snow. The times I had fallen before had been after a rush of fear—after I feared I would lose control, or feared I was going too fast, or feared I couldn't make it. Fear had always been the cause. I would not let it win now. Inhale. Exhale. You're fine, Jess. You can do this.

My life has been made up of moments of crossroads; moments where I've stood up at the top of the mountain, wondering if it's worth the risk to go down. I've always been an expert at overthinking—asking myself, Should I do this? Can I do this? What are all the things that can go wrong if I do this? Too many times in the past, I've let myself walk away. But life was not meant to be lived staying at the top of the mountain where it is safe. Life is not meant to be lived running away in fear.

I had been so focused on the precise turning of my skis that I hadn't noticed how far I'd gone until my father called out. "JESSICA!" I heard his voice from somewhere behind me. "YOU DID IT!"

I dared to look up at that moment and saw that I had, in fact, made it past the steepest part of the mountain. I couldn't believe it—I had gotten down. Pride radiating throughout my entire body, I lifted my poles into the air. As I cheered loud enough so the people on the ski lift above me could hear, I thought about the pure elation and confidence I felt at that exact moment. I could imagine the feeling of disappointment, of regret, that would've haunted me the rest of the day if I had stayed on top of the mountain and gone down a blue instead. It's safer to take the easier way out, but it's nowhere near as fun.

Fear is a natural aspect of life. I have felt it many times before, and I am sure I will feel it many times again. Having fear is not what defines me, however; I am defined by how I react to it. And I will go down the double blue every time.

Ask Dr. Jan

Dear Dr. Jan,
Have you ever been that one kid in your grade that is always different, that never seems to fit in with the grade or the school? Have you just been so different that you want to be yourself but are driven down by what people think of you?
—Nick

Dear Nick,
Yes! In fact, I think you might be surprised at how common an experience this is for many people, particularly during their teen years. We live in a society that rewards conformity and punishes differences. Despite this, I encourage people to try and maintain their individuality. They ultimately will be better off being true to themselves while learning how to deal with people who would rather see them conform.

I often hear from parents, for example, "Why can't my kid just be normal?" I always let them know to be careful what they wish for because normal really means "average." And how boring would it be to just be average?

These issues have significant potential impact on our self-image. It is true that our perception of ourselves is in part related to feedback we get from others. This is why it is so important to shift from worrying about being accepted by others to focus on being more self-accepting. It is also helpful to try and surround yourself with people who appreciate you for who you are and are not pressuring you to be someone you're not.

Hang in there. If you try to remain true to yourself despite what others may think or say, you will discover that you will have a richer and more rewarding life.

Chapter 4

Teens Talk About Finding Themselves Through Creative Expression

Creativity is a way for people to showcase their talents. When people like doing something, and do it well, it boosts their self-confidence and self-esteem. Finishing a project can make a teen feel proud of his accomplishment, which helps increase self-confidence and self-esteem.

Creativity helps people explore and share their deepest desires, fears, and aspirations. Poetry, plays, dance, music, painting, and sculpture have long served as outlets for creativity. As times change, so do the methods for expressing creativity.

Photography, knitting, and jewelry making, are popular today. So are painting parties. These group events allow participants to express themselves, reduce stress, and share their art with others. All participants paint the same thing—for instance a beach scene—but each creation is unique to the individual who painted it.

Teens who dream of dancing but think they have two left feet should remember that everyone starts as a beginner, and improvement comes in time.

That is the beauty of creative expression. It can be enjoyed privately or publicly. As such, it benefits both the creator and those who are fortunate enough to enjoy the fruits of the artist's labors. Whether or not the art is shared, creative expression aids in the development of confidence and a sense of self.

Whatever art form you choose to pursue, keep the following guidelines in mind:

Everyone is a beginner. Don't worry that your lines are crooked or your photos are blurry when you begin.

Talking about the confidence you've gained from your creative work can help a loved one dealing with issues related to self-esteem and self-confidence and may bring the two of you closer.

Expect to get better as you create, develop, and master your form.

Be authentic. Let your creativity reflect your present mood. Silence your inner critic and just pour your heart out. Enjoy the freedom that comes as you express yourself without a filter.

Someone needs that. Believe it or not, some of your friends or relatives are going through—or will go through—the same struggles that you are. Your creativity can help others grow in self-confidence and self-esteem.

Do it for yourself. Even if you share with others, create for an audience of one—yourself. Creating projects around themes or causes that are important to you will help increase your authenticity, pleasure, and pride in your work.

Presley's Story

Unlike a lot of the amazing writers on this website, I don't have an enthralling tale of tragedy and resulting growth. I had a very good childhood. One of my greatest struggles and the one I'm writing about today was, to be frank, self-inflicted. You see, I used to just plain hate myself in the most literal sense of the word. All through middle school and up until late freshmen year I despised every detail about myself. I hated my chubby tummy. I hated that I was a social outcast. I hated that I had no defining points of who I was; that is, I was average at just about everything. Sports had never been my cup of tea. I could never get into playing guitar, hard as I tried. I was, by all accounts, terribly uninteresting.

I just wanted so badly to be desirable both in looks and personality. So I began cutting. First it was just tiny slits on my thighs. Then I ran out of room, so I moved to that fat stomach I hated so much. I can't explain why I thought this was a good idea. I guess somehow carrying around this awful secret made me feel like I was finally moderately interesting.

Anyway, one thing I had always liked to do, though I was not particularly good at it, was write poetry. Just free verse, nothing fancy. I would wrap up my insecurities into cleverly disguised metaphors and similes, though I never shared them with anybody. This all changed in my late freshmen year when I took creative writing. The teacher was overwhelmingly kind and she encouraged (and sometimes forced) everybody to share their writing no matter how good or bad they felt it was. Her warm smile and genuine belief in my abilities gave me that little bit of courage I needed. I began sharing my poems first with her privately in my assignments, and then in front of the class. Their overwhelmingly positive reaction gave me that sense of belonging I had wanted for so long. I began focusing on poetry, learning new forms and techniques over the weekends so that I could share them once Monday rolled around. I stopped cutting, too. I no longer needed a dirty little secret to feel special. I had friends who thought I was genuinely fantastic. I had found my niche.

I was essentially floating on cloud nine until

Whether kept privately in a journal or shared publicly with family and friends, poetry and other written forms can help a teen express his or her thoughts and emotions.

the class ended. Then I was faced with a tough internal dilemma. Would I stop writing now that there was no audience? This also forced me to tackle a difficult question—why was I writing? Was it for myself or for the approval of others? I stopped writing poetry altogether for a short time and I felt myself being pulled back into depression.

One night, I was dangerously close to picking up that stupid pocket knife I had kept in my drawer for so many years when something else blocked that thought from my head. It was a single line, the beginning to an unwritten poem. Everything I was feeling was jammed into these few words. For the first time in months, instead of picking up a knife, I picked up a pen. I stayed up all night writing out my pain, and in my own way, dealing with it. By morning I had no new scars but one new poem. This was the beginning of something glorious.

I started writing about anything and everything. I no longer tried to fill my paper with eloquent rhyme schemes and dazzling metaphors. I wrote whatever I wanted, however it came to me naturally. I wrote out my frustrations and pains and eventually threw away that old knife. By the time junior year rolled around, my poems rarely took a melancholic tone and usually weren't even about me. Poetry was no longer something I did to impress others or to keep myself from falling back into depression. It became a way of observing and understanding the world around me, a lifestyle if you will. I shared some of my poems with others, but that was no longer the reason I was writing. They were for myself,

WHOM TO CALL

The following hotlines and organizations can help teens dealing with issues related to self-esteem and self-confidence, as well as those searching for volunteer opportunities.

Crisis Call Center
(800) 273-8255
Twenty-four hours a day, seven days a week

National Suicide Hotline
(800) 442-HOPE [4673]
Twenty-four hours a day, seven days a week

Points of Light
1-800-VOLUNTEER
http://www.pointsoflight.org
Monday through Friday, 9 a.m. to 5 p.m., EST

Thursday's Child Youth Advocacy Hotline
(800) USA-KIDS [872-5437]
Twenty-four hours a day, seven days a week

a timeless scrapbook of the things I had seen and the emotions I had felt. Life was finally good.

It took some time, but I stopped hating myself, too. I grew comfortable in my own skin, scarred at it was, and I was proud of my quiet nature and of my writing. I no longer saw myself as boring or lackluster. Sure, I wasn't as loud or as athletic as many people were at my school. But I was 100 percent me, and for once, I was okay with that. I made new friends and reconnected with old ones. It turns out many of us had the same struggles at the same time, but none of us would talk about them. Ironic, isn't it?

I would encourage anybody reading this who might be going through the same thing I was to force yourself to reach out. Isolating yourself seems to be the natural reaction to depression, but in my experience, talking it out and realizing you actually aren't alone can make you feel a thousand times better. Try and find a niche of your own, too. Maybe you can express yourself in the rhythms of the guitar or in the fervor of a soccer match like I never could. Or, maybe you'll even turn to poetry, like I did.

Whatever path you choose to take from here onward, know that you don't have to be alone, and that choosing to be comfortable in your own skin is the best decision you could ever make for your mental health. Embrace who you are and create your own meter stick to judge yourself by. Only you know the wondrous heights you are capable of obtaining.

Chapter 5

Teens Talk About Helping Others to Help Themselves

Adult volunteers provide critical help in every community. They fight fires, work at hospitals, feed the hungry, build homes, care for injured animals, and help in numerous other ways.

Millions of teens also play key roles each year by volunteering in their communities. There is always a shortage of help. It may seem impossible to volunteer when dealing with esteem or confidence issues, but helping others directly correlates with self-esteem. The more a teen cares for others, the greater her self-esteem and confidence.

Volunteering can help a teen feel more positive about himself and his ability to make a difference in society. At an understaffed shelter, the animals will be more quickly fed, walked, or groomed if that teen is there to volunteer. Kids he tutors at an after-school program will grow academically and socially. An elderly couple will have a safer walking path if he shovels their sidewalk.

Volunteering helps shape a teen's positive self-image while also contributing to the well-being of members of the local community.

When a teen sees the difference she makes in the lives of others she will begin to view herself in a more positive light. Over time the act of volunteering will improve her esteem and confidence.

Teens who want to volunteer can join an existing club or organization at school—or start a new one. They can help in the community at shelters run by nonprofit organizations like the American Society for the Prevention of Cruelty to Animals (ASPCA) or the Humane

Society of the United States. They can volunteer with youth clubs, religious organizations, and places of worship. A good place to start is to ask friends and relatives for ideas. A teacher, guidance counselor, or other trusted adult is also a great resource.

Deborah's Story

Self-esteem seemed to be that one thing that helped my friends get through breakups, bad grades, fights, anything. But for me? Oh no. Self-esteem came to me like an innocent package left for me on the front door step. Excited to see what it is, I hastily open it and all chaos breaks loose. I was never the "pretty girl" or the "smart girl." I mean, I didn't feel that bad because I was probably grouped under the umbrella considered "the other girl" that included 70 percent of the girls in the student population.

However, the drive on the smooth road came to an end, and all of a sudden my life was trying to drive up a steep mountain, but all in vain. This was the beginning of middle school. Because I moved houses in between elementary and middle school, I was forced to move schools, also. And thus it began, the unprecedented chaos. Suddenly I felt like a victim wherever I went. When any pair of eyes would set on me, I would suddenly curl into a ball, hoping I would be less visible. When people talked to me, I would never answer. I mean, better not to answer when they are ultimately going to judge me, right? I would come home and cry myself to sleep every day wondering what it was about me that made me a loser. And I would answer "everything."

I was treated worse than anyone. I mean imagine a one-eyed alien that looked like Stitch (from *Lilo and Stitch*) and Mike Wazowski (*Monsters Inc.*) came to your school. I bet you that I was treated worse than any crazy monster that such a fantasy can come up with. I mean at least Stitch had Lilo and Mike had James P. Sullivan. Me? No one. I spent my days eating by myself in the corner of the school. I would anxiously wait, and

Eating alone is no fun, but low self-esteem and lack of self-confidence can make it difficult to interact with other teens throughout the school day.

when it felt like no one was there, I would eat my lunch in basically two gulps because I didn't want people to see me committing the deeds that basically defined a loser. And eighth grade didn't help much, either. Now it was the facial blemishes that brought me down lower, if that was even possible. To hide these monsters, I would apply foundation so thick that I probably scared off people with my "outstanding" coverage.

To top it off, I was the school's scapegoat. Did you do something wrong? No problem. Deborah was the go-to girl for blaming your faults on. Were you worried that you might get caught? Not one bit, because Deborah was too scared and would rather deal with the consequences than look bad in front of her peers another time. It got to the point where my so-called "best friend" would talk bad about my other "best friend," and then when the girl found out, suddenly the blame's on me. Bewildered beyond anything, I would just stare and look hopelessly, and not even try to defend myself because… even if I did, would anyone listen to me?

But then, this is the good part. The part when my drive up the mountain is finally a walk through the garden. Not a perfect one though; it still has bees that bring the occasional sting. I began to volunteer. Now as corny as that sounds, volunteering was self-healing for me. I finally found a place where I was able to have my love reciprocated. Love that could be expressed with just the eyes. This volunteer organization was created to help single parents, and my job was to teach the kids music and art, two of my most passionate subjects. The art portion was called "art therapy," and art was therapy,

Helping others is a win-win situation. Those you help get the benefit of your expertise, and you find a positive outlet that can counteract any negative feelings about yourself.

at least for me. By helping others, I was able to escape my problems, at least for those few hours. I was finally able to swim in the deep end, and the few seconds of air I could take in before my head was back in the water were so sweet and memorable.

As a high school student, I am still volunteering and feel blessed to have gone through such a horrid experience. Because when I see people in school that seem to be another victim of the ugly side of self-esteem, I immediately, without having to think, show them that I love them. And although this seems like the most selfless act, I have to admit it is a selfish deed, if

I consider it. Selfish because in the end I am healing myself because I am proving to myself that I am in the position to love others, although my self-esteem may tell me otherwise.

Alexandra's Story

I can't remember how it started, but I wouldn't be here today if it didn't end. Like every other teenager I was discovering myself in middle school. I participated in soccer and even the school play, but somehow, somewhere I was feeling more and more insecure about my appearance and who I was as a person. I actually was very close to getting an eating disorder. It started with skipping lunch every day and then breakfast slowly went away too. I was so hungry by dinner time I would eat double a normal portion, and then feel like I defeated the whole purpose of not eating—and then continue the whole process the next day. What made it worse was not even my parents realized I was doing this, and when friends did notice I made up little stories about how I had already eaten. I always promised myself that I'd never do that, but somehow I was getting closer to a disorder every day.

One day after the performance of our school play a little girl approached me. I've always had a fondness for children, and I dropped to one knee to talk to her. She shyly asked to see the princess who was portrayed by one of my friends in the play. When I showed her where the princess was she simply looked at me and said, "No. You the princess." Even when I had just a small part as a village girl in the play.

For days I pondered what this little girl had said. Was I truly a princess and really not willing to accept myself for who I was? That day I began to eat a little breakfast and a little more each day until I returned to a healthy diet.

I'm proud to say that as a freshman student I have fully returned to a normal diet and continue to share the importance of self-esteem with students. I want them to know that they are beautiful and should accept themselves for who they are rather than give up eating to reach some idea of perfection. Because of my experience I've hosted an event for younger Girl Scouts that improves their self-esteem so they won't end up the way I was—struggling with almost having an eating disorder.

My advice to anyone in my situation would be to tell someone, and if you can't do that make a list of everything you find beautiful about yourself. I also love to write poetry and find it a great way to express my feelings.

Never stopping searching for help, because as a little girl showed me, help can be offered in millions of different ways.

10 Great Questions
to Ask a Guidance Counselor

1. Why should I care about improving my self-esteem and self-confidence?

2. Can you give me strategies for sharing my self-esteem issues with my family?

3. My self-esteem was fine until I hit puberty. Does that mean I have to wait until puberty is over to raise my self-esteem and self-confidence?

4. How do I confidently share my talents without getting a reputation as someone who always brags or has a big head?

5. Why does it seem like my self-esteem goes in cycles, where sometimes I'm okay and sometimes I'm not?

6. Some of my relatives have suffered from poor self-esteem all of their life. Is there any hope that I can improve mine?

7. How can I protect myself from cyberbullying?

8. How can I build new friendships after changing schools because I was bullied?

9. What are the warning signs that someone might be thinking about self-harm?

10. Can diet and exercise affect my self-esteem and self-confidence?

The Teen Health & Wellness Personal Story Project

Be part of the Teen Health & Wellness Personal Story Project and share your story about successfully dealing with or overcoming a challenge. If your story is accepted for online publication, it will be posted on the Teen Health & Wellness site and featured on its homepage. You will also receive a certificate of achievement from Rosen Publishing and a $25 gift certificate to Barnes & Noble or Chapters.

Sharing stories is a powerful way to connect with other people. By sharing your story, you can connect with others who are dealing with these challenges. Visit teenhealthandwellness.com/static/personalstoryproject to read other teens' stories and to submit your own.

Scan this QR code to go to the Personal Story Project homepage.

Glossary

acquiesce To agree with or submit to someone else's opinions or desires.

adage A wise saying or proverb that is familiar to many people.

authentic Reflective of a person's true values and beliefs.

browbeat To talk sternly in order to intimidate, frighten, or threaten someone.

chaos A lack of order or control; total confusion.

coerce To force or pressure someone to do something.

contagious Easily spread from one person to another.

empathy The ability to relate to another person's emotions or experiences because you have experienced similar situations.

deride To mock or ridicule a person.

dumbfounded So surprised and amazed as to be left speechless.

flabbergasted Being surprised, amazed, or stunned by something or someone.

impromptu Anything that is unplanned, such as an action, speech, or event.

mimic To imitate or copy another person's actions or words.

phobia A deep-rooted fear of someone, or something, whether real or imaginary.

resilience The ability to rediscover success in an area after a setback.

scrutinizing Analyzing or examining closely, usually in a negative way.

self-esteem A healthy sense of confidence in one's worth as a person.

stellar Anything that is outstanding or terrific.

stifle To restrain or suppress an action or emotion.

suicide The act of killing oneself.

treacherous An unsafe, dangerous, or harmful condition.

unprecedented Something that has never been done before.

vulnerable To be weak, helpless, or defenseless.

For More Information

AnxietyBC
311-409 Granville St
Vancouver, BC V6C 1T2
Canada
Telephone: (604) 620-0744
Website: https://www.anxietybc.com
Facebook: @AnxietyBC
Twitter: @AnxietyBC
Youtube: https://www.youtube.com/user/AnxietyBC
This Canadian nonprofit offers resources to help teens develop a plan to cope with anxiety disorders.

Big Brothers Big Sisters of America
2202 N. Westshore Boulevard, Suite 455
Tampa, FL 33607
Telephone: (813) 720-8778
Website: https://www.bbbs.org
Facebook: @BigBrothersBigSisters
Twitter: @BBBSA
Youtube: https://www.youtube.com/user/BBBSofAmerica
Big Brothers Big Sisters of America matches youth participants with a personal mentor who helps guide, motivate, and encourage them.

Girls Inc.
120 Wall Street
New York, NY 10005-3902

Telephone: (212) 509-2000
Website: http://www.girlsinc.org
Facebook: @GirlsInc
Twitter:@girls_inc
Instagram: @girlsinc
Girls' Inc. focuses on providing programs, mentoring, and other resources to help girls grow up to be strong, independent, involved citizens.

Kids Help Phone
300-439 University Avenue
Toronto, ON M5G 1Y8
Telephone: (416) 586-5437; (800) 268-3062
Website: http://org.kidshelpphone.ca
Facebook: @KidsHelpPhone
Twitter: @KidsHelpPhone
Kids Help Phone offers Canadian youth confidential, anonymous counseling services. It provides online counseling, games, an app, and websites for children and teens, as well as an interactive resource for finding local services.

Pacer's National Bullying Prevention Center
Minneapolis Office:
Pacer Center, Inc.
8161 Normandale Boulevard
Bloomington, MN 55437
Los Angeles Office
Pacer's National Bullying Prevention Center
2953 Lincoln Blvd.
Santa Monica, CA 90405

Telephone: (952) 838-9000 or (800) 537-2237
Website: http://www.pacer.org/bullying/about/contact.asp
Facebook: PACERsNationalBullyingPreventionCenter
Pacer's National Bullying Prevention Center provides
  videos, school kits, activities, and other material to
  help students, parents, educators, and others identity
  and prevent bullying.

Teen Health and Wellness
29 East 21st Street
New York, NY 10010
Telephone: (877) 381-6649
Website: http://www.teenhealthandwellness.com
Teen Health & Wellness provides nonjudgmental,
  straightforward, curricular and self-help support on
  topics such as diseases, drugs and alcohol, nutrition,
  mental health, suicide and bullying, green living, and
  LGBTQ issues. Its free Teen Hotlines app provides a
  concise list of hotlines, help lines, and information
  lines on the subjects that affect teens most.

Volunteer Canada
275 Bank Street, Suite 400
Ottawa, ON K2P 2L6
Canada
Telephone: (800) 670-0401
Website: https://www.volunteer.ca
Facebook: @VolunteerCanada
Twitter: @VolunteerCanada
Volunteer Canada works to increase and support
  volunteerism and civic participation in Canada.

Volunteer Match
550 Montgomery Street, 8th Floor
San Francisco, CA 94111
Website: https://www.volunteermatch.org
Facebook: @VolunteerMatch
Twitter: @VolunteerMatch
Youtube: https://www.youtube.com/user/
    VolunteerMatch
Volunteer Match helps people match their interests with
    organizations seeking volunteers.

Websites

Because of the changing nature of internet links, Rosen
Publishing has developed an online list of websites
related to the subject of this book. This site is updated
regularly. Please use this link to access this list:

http://www.rosenlinks.com/TNV/Self

For Further Reading

Borus, Audrey. *Volunteering: A How-to Guide*. Berkeley Heights, NJ: Enslow, 2012.

Bradshaw, Cheryl. *How to Like Yourself: A Teen's Guide to Quieting Your Inner Critic and Building Lasting Self-Esteem*. Oakland, CA: Instant Help Books, 2016.

Byers, Ann. *Internship & Volunteer Opportunities for People Who Love Animals* (A Foot in the Door). New York, NY: Rosen Publishing, 2013.

Cain, Susan. *Quiet Power: The Secret Strengths of Introverts*. New York, NY: Dial Books for Young Readers, 2016.

Covey, Sean. *The 7 Habits of Highly Effective Teens*. New York, NY: Touchstone, 2014.

Meyer, Jared. *Making Friends* (Communicating with Confidence). New York, NY: Rosen Publishing, 2012.

Morrison, Ben, and Ruth Ruiz. *Self-Esteem* (Teen Mental Health). New York, NY: Rosen Publishing, 2012.

Penn, Maya S. *You Got This!: Unleash Your Awesomeness, Find Your Path, and Change Your World*. New York, NY: North Star Way, 2016.

Schwartz, Heather E. *Stress Less: Your Guide to Managing Stress*. Mankato, MN: Capstone Press, 2012.

Thompson, Laurie Ann. *Be a Changemaker: How to Start Something That Matters*. New York, NY: Simon Pulse/Beyond Words, 2013.

Winkler, Kathleen. *Are You Being Bullied?* (Got Issues?). Berkeley Heights, NJ: Enslow, 2014.

Bibliography

"Alexandra's Story." Teen Health and Wellness, April 2017. http://www.teenhealthandwellness.com /article/292/14/alexandras-story.

American Psychological Association. "American Psychological Association Survey Shows Teen Stress Rivals That of Adults." February 11, 2014. www.apa .org/news/press/releases/2014/02/teen-stress.aspx.

"Anh's Story." Teen Health and Wellness, April 2017. http://www.teenhealthandwellness.com /article/292/16/anhs-story.

Child Development Institute. "How to Help Children and Teens Develop Healthy Self-Esteem." March 25, 2017. https://childdevelopmentinfo.com /child-psychology/self-esteem/#.WPgA_rvHc5s.

"Deborah's Story." Teen Health and Wellness, April 2017. http://www.teenhealthandwellness.com /article/292/15/deborahs-story.

"Emoijah's Story." Teen Health and Wellness, April 2017. http://www.teenhealthandwellness.com /article/292/19/emoijahs-story.

"Jessica's Story." Teen Health and Wellness, April 2017. http://www.teenhealthandwellness.com /article/292/17/jessicas-story.

"Kenna's Story." Teen Health and Wellness, April 2017. http://www.teenhealthandwellness.com /article/292/8/kennas-story.

Kids Health "How Can I Improve My Self-Esteem." Retrieved March 25, 2017.

http://kidshealth.org/en/teens/self-esteem.html?WT
.ac=t-ra.

Lock, Cheryl. "Turn to the Arts to Boost Self-Esteem."
PBS Parents, March 26, 2017.
www.pbs.org/parents/education/music-arts/
turn-to-the-arts-to-boost-self-esteem.

"Meg's Story." Teen Health and Wellness, April 2017.
http://www.teenhealthandwellness.com/article/292/9
/megs-story.

"Natalie's Story." Teen Health and Wellness, April 2017.
http://www.teenhealthandwellness.com/article/76/15
/natalies-story.

National Bullying Prevention Center. Accessed March
25, 2017. http://pacer.org/bullying.

Nelson, Maria. *I Can Volunteer.* New York, NY: Gareth
Stevens Publishing, 2014.

Pompa, Frank. "Teens Feeling Stressed, and Many Not
Managing It Well." *USA Today,* February 11, 2014.
www.usatoday.com/story/news/nation/2014/02/11
/stress-teens-psychological/5266739.

"Presley's Story." Teen Health and Wellness, April 2017.
http://www.teenhealthandwellness.com
/article/292/18/presleys-story.

Stevens, Christiana. "New National Survey Finds Nearly
Half of Teenagers Stressed Out." *Global News,*
September 15, 2015. http://globalnews.ca/
news/2222718
/new-national-survey-finds-nearly-half-of-teenagers
-stressed-out.

Zelinger, Laura. *A Smart Girl's Guide to Liking Herself—
Even on the Bad Days.* Middleton, WI: American
Girl, 2012.

Index

A

areas to work on, 6, 9, 20
Ask Dr. Jan, 34

B

benefits of improved
    self-esteem and self-
    confidence, 6, 7
bullying, 8, 9, 14, 15

C

confidence issues, 5, 7, 43
creative expression, 35–37
  personal story, 38
creativity, 35, 37
criticism, 6, 9, 10
cutting, 7, 38, 39

E

effects of low self-esteem
    and self-confidence,
    6–7

F

fear, 6, 14, 17, 26, 27, 28,
    32, 33, 35

fear, facing of, 26–27
  personal stories, 27, 31
  stage fright, 28–29

H

help hotlines, 41
helping others to help your-
    self, 43–45
  personal stories, 45, 49

M

myths and facts, 18

N

negative self-image, over-
    coming, 19–20
  personal stories, 21, 23
  taking positive steps, 20

O

outer appearances, 19

Q

questions to ask, 51

About the Editor

Jennifer Landau is an author and editor who has written about psychological bullying, cybercitizenship, and drug and alcohol abuse, among other topics. She has an MA in English from New York University and an MST in general and special education from Fordham University. Landau has taught writing to young children, teens, and seniors.

About Dr. Jan

Dr. Jan Hittelman, a licensed psychologist with over thirty years experience working with children and families, has authored monthly columns for the *Daily Camera,* Boulder Valley School District, and online for Rosen Publishing Group. He is the founder of the Boulder Counseling Cooperative and the director of Boulder Psychological Services.

Photo Credits